We Read
PHONICS™

Bugs on the Bus

TREASURE BAY

Parent's Introduction

Welcome to **We Read Phonics**! This series is designed to help you assist your child in reading. Each book includes a story, as well as some simple word games to play with your child. The games focus on the phonics skills and sight words your child will use in reading the story.

Here are some recommendations for using this book with your child:

1 Word Play

There are word games both before and after the story. Make these games fun and playful. If your child becomes bored or frustrated, play a different game or take a break.

Phonics is a method of sounding out words by blending together letter sounds. However, not all words can be "sounded out." **Sight words** are frequently used words that usually cannot be sounded out.

② Read the Story

After some word play, read the story aloud to your child—or read the story together, by reading aloud at the same time or by taking turns. As you and your child read, move your finger under the words.

Next, have your child read the entire story to you while you follow along with your finger under the words. If there is some difficulty with a word, either help your child to sound it out or wait about five seconds and then say the word.

③ Discuss and Read Again

After reading the story, talk about it with your child. Ask questions like, "What happened in the story?" and "What was the best part?" It will be helpful for your child to read this story to you several times. Another great way for your child to practice is by reading the book to a younger sibling, a pet, or even a stuffed animal!

And then what happened?

All the bugs escaped!

LEVEL ② **Level 2** introduces simple words with short "e," short "o," and short "u" (as in *get, hot,* and *bug*). All consonants except "q" are used at this level. Special sounds include "ck" (as in *lock*), "wh" (as in *when*), "ar" (as in *car*), and "s" as the "z" sound (as in *bugs*).

Bugs on the Bus

A We Read Phonics™ Book
Level 2

Text Copyright © 2010 by Treasure Bay, Inc.
Illustrations Copyright © 2010 by Michele Noiset

Reading Consultants: Bruce Johnson, M.Ed., and Dorothy Taguchi, Ph.D.

We Read Phonics™ is a trademark of Treasure Bay, Inc.

Published by
Treasure Bay, Inc.
P.O. Box 119
Novato, CA 94948 USA

Printed in Singapore

Library of Congress Catalog Card Number: 2009929511

Hardcover ISBN: 978-1-60115-325-8
Paperback ISBN: 978-1-60115-326-5
PDF E-Book ISBN: 978-1-60115-580-1

We Read Phonics™
Patent Pending

Visit us online at:
www.TreasureBayBooks.com

PR-1-12

Bugs on the Bus

By Paul Orshoski and D. J. Panec

Illustrated by Michele Noiset

Phonics Game

Creating words using certain letters will help your child read this story.

Alphabet Soup

Materials:

Option 1—Fast and Easy: To print the game materials from your computer, go online to www.WeReadPhonics.com, then go to this book title and click on the link to "View & Print: Game Materials."

Option 2—Make Your Own: You'll need paper or cardboard, markers, a small cooking pot and a stirring spoon. Cut 2 x 2 inch squares from the paper or cardboard and print these letters on the squares: e, o, u, a, ar, ck, wh, g, b, s, c, k, j, l, t, m, p, n, f, r, w, *and* h.

1 One player takes the letter "e." The other player takes the letter "u." Place the other letters into a pretend pot of soup.

2 Players stir the letters. Each player takes a letter from the pot. Stir again. Each player takes another letter. When a player can make a word by putting his letters together, he makes and reads the word out loud.

3 Continue stirring. Each player continues to take additional letters and make words.

4 For a second game, the child can start with the letter "o" and the letter combination "ck," and the parent can start with the letter "e" and the letter combination "wh."

Words that can be made with these letters include *bugs, bus, back, sock, jar, lot, get, jump, whack, wet, crack,* and *when.*

Sight Word Game

Memory

This is a fun way to practice recognizing some sight words used in the story.

Materials:

Option 1—Fast and Easy: To print the game materials from your computer, go online to www.WeReadPhonics.com, then go to this book title and click on the link to "View & Print: Game Materials."

Option 2—Make Your Own: You'll need 18 index cards and a marker. Write each word listed on the right on two cards. You will now have two sets of cards.

1 Using one set of cards, ask your child to repeat each word after you. Shuffle both decks of cards together, and arrange the cards face down in a grid pattern.

2 The first player turns over one card and says the word, then turns over a second card and says the word. If the cards match, the player takes those cards and continues to play. If they don't match, both cards are turned over, and it's the next player's turn.

3 Keep the cards. You can make more cards with other **We Read Phonics** books and combine the cards for even bigger games!

this

there

the

makes

with

of

oh

for

where

This is Gus.

This is his bus.

I am Jack.

I sit in the back.

There are lots
of big bugs . . .

. . . in a jar that I lug.

Oh, no! There is Bill.

Bill sits where he will.

The bus hits a bump.

The jar gets a whack.

I jump for the jar.

The jar gets a crack.

Bill slaps at a bug.

Bill slaps and he smacks.

So, a bug bit his hand.

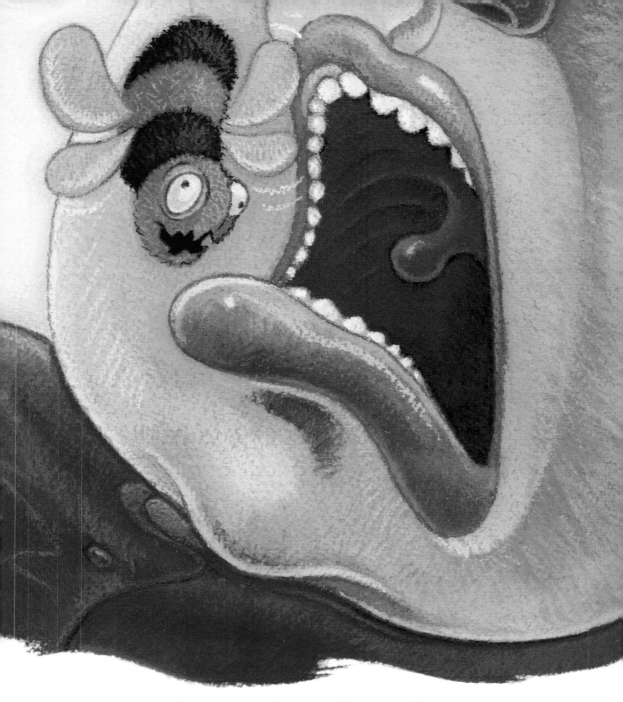

A bug bit his lip.

A bug bit his neck.

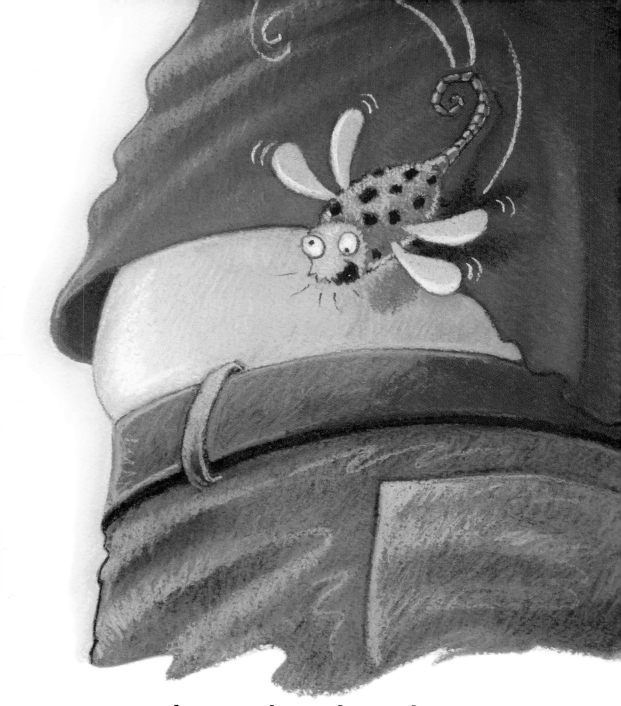

A bug bit his hip.

Bill makes a big fuss.

And Gus stops the bus.

Bill yells and he frets…

…and jumps and gets wet.

Rhyming

Practicing rhyming words helps children learn how words are similar.

Can you think of another word that rhymes with wet?

Not yet!

1. Explain to your child that these words rhyme because they have the same end sounds: *bug, chug, dug, hug, jug, lug, mug, pug, rug,* and *tug.*

2. Ask your child to say a word that rhymes with *bug.*

3. If your child has trouble, offer some possible answers or repeat step 1. It's okay to accept nonsense words, for example, *cug.*

4. When your child is successful, repeat step 2 with these words:

   jar   (possible answers: *bar, car, far, par, star, tar*)

   Jack (possible answers: *back, clack, pack, rack, sack, stack, tack*)

   Bill   (possible answers: *fill, gill, hill, Jill, mill, sill, still, will*)

   lot   (possible answers: *cot, got, hot, jot, not, pot, rot*)

   top   (possible answers: *bop, cop, drop, flop, hop, mop, pop, stop*)

   sit   (possible answers: *bit, fit, hit, lit, mitt, pit, wit*)

Phonics Game

Taking a Trip

Recognizing first letter sounds helps readers learn to read new words.

Can you think of any words that start with the sound "b"?

Bat and ball!

1. Explain to your child that the words *smile, Sam,* and *silly* all begin with the sound "s." (Instead of saying the letter, make the sound for "s.")

2. Say: "I am taking a trip. You can join me if you can think of a word that begins with the sound 's.' (Make the sound for 's.') Can you think of a word that begins with the sound 's'?" Correct answers can include words from the book or words outside of the book that begin with the "s" sound.

3. If your child has trouble, offer some possible answers or repeat step 1.

4. When your child is successful, repeat step 2 with these beginning sounds: c, m, l, h, b, g, j, k, y, *and* w.

If you liked *Bugs on the Bus,*
here is another **We Read Phonics** book you are sure to enjoy!

Which Pet Is Best?

Choosing a pet can be really hard. Some are cute, most are fun, and all of them are so interesting! Join a young girl on a trip through a pet shop in this amusing and easy-to-read book for beginning readers!